"There are certain areas of feeling and reality—or unreality or innermost yearning, whatever you want to call it—which are notably inaccessible to words. Music can get into these areas. Painting can get into them. Non-verbal forms of expression can. There's a side to the human personality that somehow senses that wherever the cosmic truth may lie, it doesn't lie in A, B, C, D. It lies somewhere in the mysterious, unknowable aspects of thought and life and experience."

Stanley Kubrick

Life Changing Classics, Volume IV
That Something

Published by
Executive Books
206 West Allen Street
Mechanicsburg, PA 17055
717-766-9499
800-233-2665
Fax: 717-766-6565
www.executivebooks.com

Illustrations on pages 42, 43, 60, 118-121, 139, 148-159,
and the inside front and back by Alberti.

Old Master imagery licensed courtesy of
Chroma Technologies, LLC.

ISBN: 978-1-933715-69-8

Printed in China

2 3 4 5 6 7 8 9

www.iconicbooks.com

Once you find it,
your life will never be the same!

That Something

William W. Woodbridge

Foreword by Paul J. Meyer

dedicated to:

that something within

4

Foreword by Paul J. Meyer

Over a half century ago,
I was given this story in a little booklet
--- with no author and no address.

I don't remember who gave it to me,
but I do remember that he suggested
I read and reread it.

When I began reading this story,
I just couldn't put it down.

My suggestion to you
is the same I received:
Read and reread it!

Scenes

page 32

page 60

page 136

a long

This happened
Time ago.

I never see a man limp
without thinking
of that day.

The sky
wept.

The

No rift
of brighter color broke
the drabness of it.

I thought the Universe wept.
That was my outlook.

Universe
wept.

The very times were in misery.
Men were out of work.

I was one of them.

Men were in

Mise

I had slept the night before on the
cold, cement floor of the city's jail.
I slept as a tired dog sleeps, a dog
worn out with a fruitless chase.

All of the night before, I had walked,
walked, walked—my pride keeping
me from this place. And so the day
had found me walking, aimlessly,
looking only for food, shelter
and work.

This could not last forever, so that
night I had stumbled down the low,
narrow hallway of the jail, and been
let into a barred cell with a hundred
others. And there I had lain as one
dead, on the cold, hard floor.

But it is of the day
that followed
that night in jail
that you shall hear.

For that was the day of my life.
It was then that I found
"THAT SOMETHING."

It was
then that
I found...

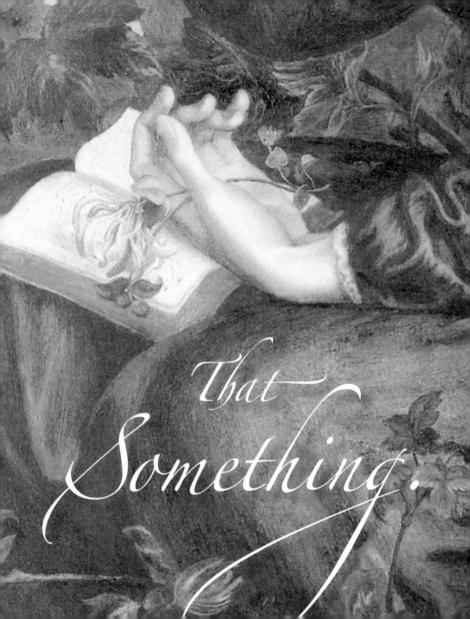

That
Something.

My feet were very tired.
My soul wept with the sky.

I stood,
as in a wilderness alone,
on the corner of a
great thoroughfare in a
great city.

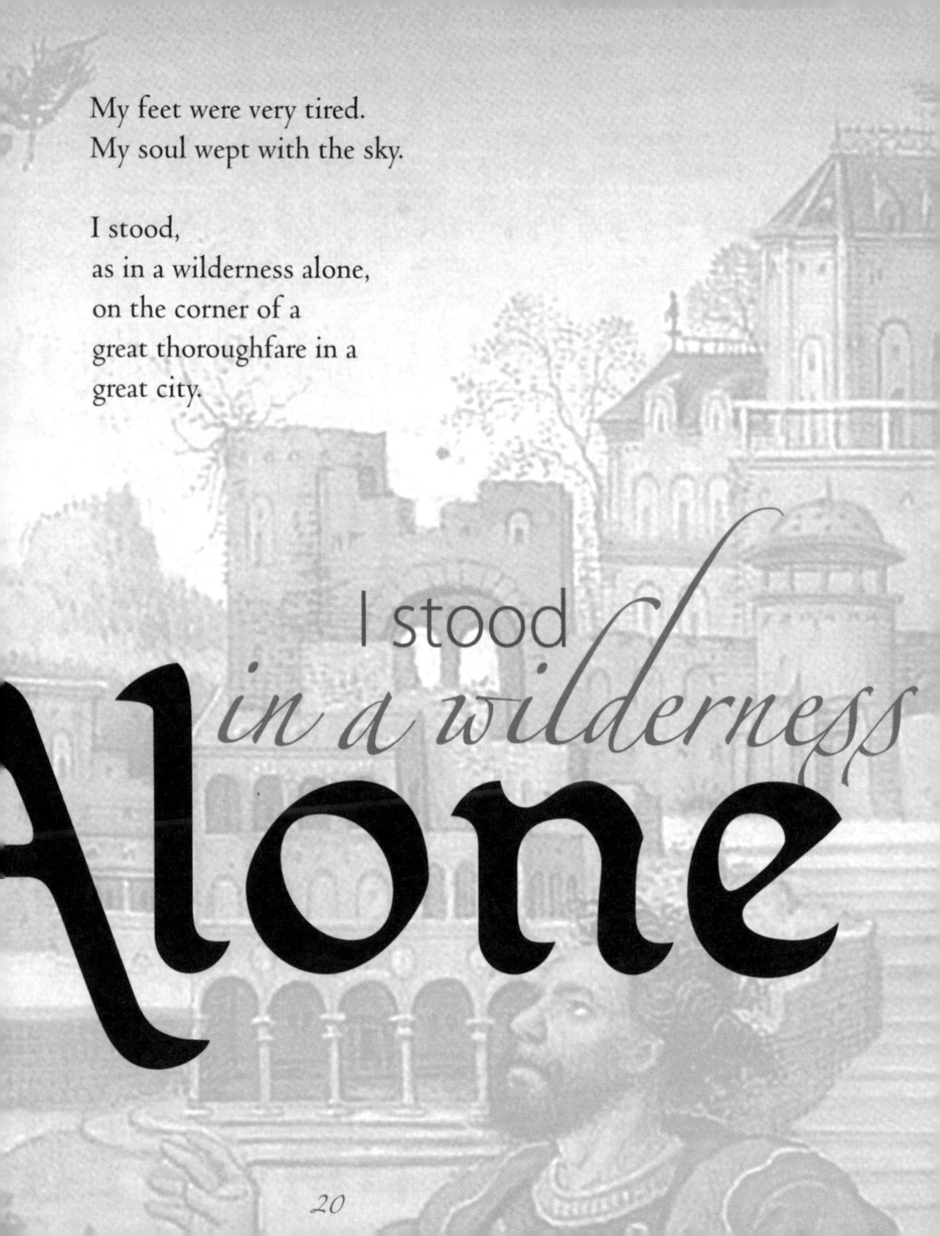

I stood
in a wilderness
Alone

Psalmi penitentiales

And then a man
stopped by my side.
He was of my height and build.

I caught a glimpse of his face.
I thought that this man might
have been myself, if—

my
search

But my present need drove out
reflections. And so I laid
my hand on his arm.

"I am hungry," I said simply.

He turned slowly and looked at me.
First his gaze took in every detail
of the outer man, from water soaked
cap to my poor, cracked shoes.

And then through my eyes,
he seemed to search my soul.

I stood there abashed.
I laugh when I think of that now.

But then—it was different.

laugh

when I think of it now.

¿help me?

No

Nobody wants men now.

"Well," he said presently,
"suppose you were fed. What then?"

I shifted my weight
from one tired foot to the other.

"I'd try to get a job somewhere,"
I muttered after a moment.

"You'd try?" he asked.

"Yes, try" I answered, "although there
is little chance. Nobody wants men
now. I'll try, sir. But I don't care
for that now. It's food I want.
I'm hungry. Can you help me?"

go find that

"No," he answered,
 a note of pity in his voice.
"I cannot help you. No man can."

"But you could feed me" I said,
 with some petulance in my voice.

"It is not food that you need!"
"What then?" I asked.

"THAT SOMETHING,"
was his reply.

when you find it

ome to me

A man joined him.
They began talking of
matters of mutual interest.

I was shuffling away through
the drizzling, miserable rain,
when he called me back,
and handed me his card.

"Man, go find
"THAT SOMETHING," he said,
"and when you've found it,
come to me."

"Come to you for what?" I asked.

"To thank me," was his answer,
and he and his friend passed on.

I believe in miracles.
There used to be such things.

Man has been taught
to work the miracles of today.
He gives them another name.

But they are miracles,
just the same.

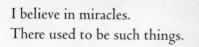

I believe in Mir

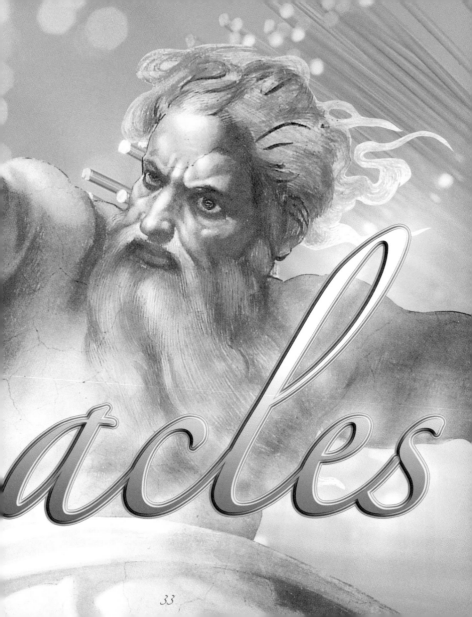

acles

There were two words
that stuck in my memory.
"THAT SOMETHING."

I fell to wondering.
I turned into a pool room,
and found a seat.

I sat there thinking.

The balls on the tables before me
clicked nickels away from men
who could ill afford the
pleasures of the place.

I sat there a long, long time.
There was nowhere else to go.

Nowhere

Ahead of me I saw
another night in jail.

Yet the day seemed longer
than the night.

It was warm in there.

The hum of voices, the regular
click, click, click of ivory,
the occasional thumping of cue
on marble floor—
all this in time developed
into a dull chorus of monotony.

And then I fell asleep.

else to go

I believe in God.
I believe in miracles.
I believe in visions as well.

But it is only natural
that I should have dreamed of
"THAT SOMETHING"—
so perhaps it was
neither miracle
nor vision.

36

I believe in God

Recognize

You will think it a foolish dream.
Yet it changed my life.

That's reason enough
for the telling.

You may laugh at it scornfully.

Then my dream
will do you no good.

You may see in it what I saw.

Then you will *take your place*
with the masters.

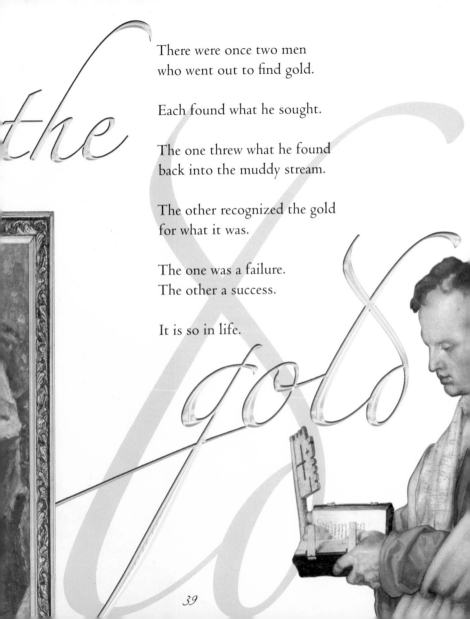

There were once two men
who went out to find gold.

Each found what he sought.

The one threw what he found
back into the muddy stream.

The other recognized the gold
for what it was.

The one was a failure.
The other a success.

It is so in life.

And this was my dream:
I dreamed that I awoke!

That is the most wonderful part
of the dream. For in my dream,
I realized that I had been asleep.

A long, long sleep,
from the very beginning of things.

And I saw myself,
there in the pool room,
asleep.

hidden in

Then I saw myself start,
my eyes opened and
I dreamed that I saw.

"What waked me?"
I asked in my dream.

"You waked yourself,"
answered a voice nearby.

I turned about,
but no one was near.
"Who are you?" I asked.

"I am 'THAT SOMETHING,'"
came the reply.

But where are you?

your soul

I am

For some moments I thought over what was said. "How," I stammered then, "how did you get there?"

"I was born there."

"Why have I not known you were there before?"

"No man knows it," answered the voice, "until he awakes."

¿ Design a priesthood?

You are

Faith.

ACE THE GOLIATHS

"No man?" I asked.
"Are you in other souls as well?"

"There is '**THAT SOMETHING**'
in everyone's soul, which can move
the mountains or dry the seas."

"Then," said I, "you must be Faith!"

"Yes," came the answer, "I am Faith,
but I am more than Faith. I am that
which helps you face the Goliaths
of your Life, and win."

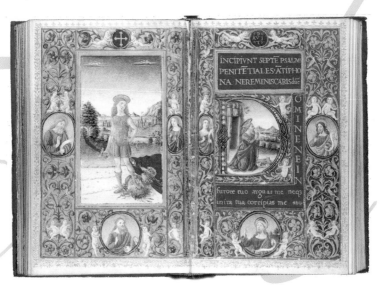

45

You are

Confidence

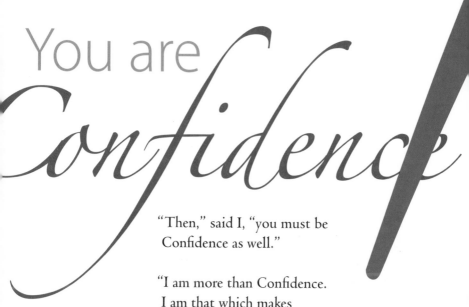

"Then," said I, "you must be
Confidence as well."

"I am more than Confidence.
I am that which makes
the babbling brooks
lift worlds upon
their wavelets."

you are Power!

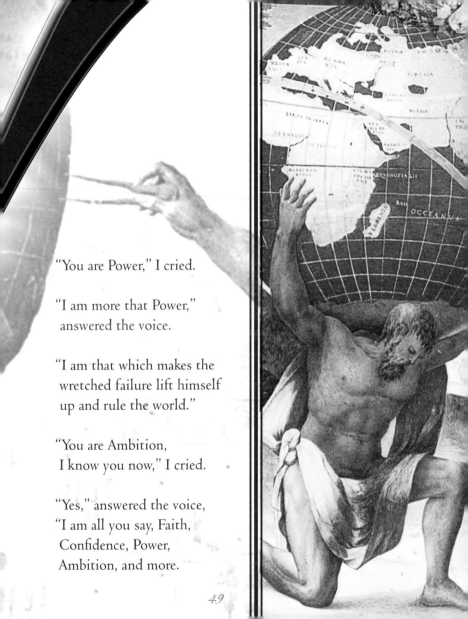

"You are Power," I cried.

"I am more that Power,"
 answered the voice.

"I am that which makes the
 wretched failure lift himself
 up and rule the world."

"You are Ambition,
 I know you now," I cried.

"Yes," answered the voice,
 "I am all you say, Faith,
 Confidence, Power,
 Ambition, and more.

49

ontrol

You

For greater than all is
THAT SOMETHING.

I am that which every man must
find in his soul, or else he will be
but a clutter of the earth
on which he lives."

"But how can we find you?"

"Even as you are finding me now,"
came the answer. "First you must
awake, then seek, and when you
have found, you must learn
to control———"

"Control what?" I asked,
confused.

must learn to

Something.

"THAT SOMETHING,"
came the reply.

"Borrow it from your soul
and baptize your life with it.

Anoint your eyes,
that you may SEE!

Anoint your ears,
that you may HEAR!

Anoint your heart,
that you may BE!"

ΤΟΝ ΑΥΤΟΥ. ΠΕΡΙ ΦΙΛΟΠΤΩΧΙΑС·

ὑδρῶ ἀδελφοὶ
καὶ οἰμωθῆη
τὸ· ἀποχοιτὸρ
ἄπαται τὸ λαὶ
τῆς θείας χαὶ
ριτος βωδεεῖς·
λίαν ἄλλος ἄλ
λου τωροδχειμ

δοκιμειροῖο
μέτροισμέτρ
μύρος·δδξαο
τὸμ· ὑβρὶ φιλ
πωχίαο λόγ
μήωθμιχ
ἄλλ ἀφιλο τ
μοος· ἱραιια

54

"But tell me," I cried, frantically for the voice was trailing off to almost nothing, "how can I do this? How? How?"

"This is the secret,"
came the voice to me as the whisper of a gentle breeze of springtime, "the talisman of success, which write upon your memory in letters of fire."

"Yes! Yes! What is the talisman?"

THIS IS THE מָשָׁל

"These words, 'I WILL.'"

"I will."

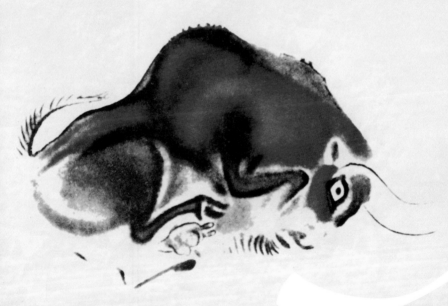

And then I awoke with a start.
A man was shaking me roughly.

"Clean out of here," he was saying.
"We ain't running no free rooming
house for bums. If you want to sleep,
take a sleeper, but get out of here."

"I will," I answered unthinkingly, as I
turned towards the door of the place.
"I WILL."

"I will."

My words brought the dream back
to me vividly. I stood in the doorway,
peering out into the rain. A boy with
a dozen bundles stopped near me
to shift his load.

"I'll help you, son," I said,
and I laughed gladly as I took half
his load and started with him
down the street.

"Gee mister," he said, "dat's pretty
square of you, all right. How far
you going, this way?"

"*Where are you* taking these things?"
I asked. He told me.

"Why, that's right where I'm going,"
I answered, in mock surprise.
And so we hurried
on our way.

Where

are you going?

Alberti

60

It was then the clouds overhead began to break. Before we had gone half way, the sun peeped out, and the boy by my side laughed with the pure delight of it.

"By Golly, mister, she's going to be some handsome day tomorrow, ain't it?"

"I WILL," I answered absently.

He looked up at me, startled at my answer, started to ask a question, thought better of it, and giving me another queer look, trudged on in silence.

"I WILLO

When he had delivered his packages, he turned back towards the thoroughfare; and, as I followed, he asked me, with the innocent impertinence of boyhood: "Say, mister, where do you work?"

"Why, I'm working for you, right now. It's good to work, don't you think?"

"But ain't you got no steady job"?"

"Yes," I answered firmly, "I WILL."

Again he cast at me his queer look, and quickened his pace.

We went together to the store at which he worked. It was the largest in the city. We hurried through a doorway at the rear, and I found myself in a large room.

A man stepped up to me and asked what I wanted.

"I have come here to work."

"What department?" he asked. *"Who sent you?"*

There were many men in there, packing boxes. Before I could answer his question, someone called him, and he hurried away.

I took off my coat, hung it on a nail near where the other men had hung theirs. I started to work, following the example of those near me.

64

ואהבת
לרעך
כמוך

Who

sent you?

65

DO YOUR BEST

A half hour later,
the man who first accosted me passed.

"Oh," he said,
as he paused behind me, "so they put
you at it while I was gone, did they?"

"*I'm doing my best*, sir," I answered
as I drove a nail home with a bang.

66

And so I worked until six o'clock.
And the sun was very bright outside.

When the six o'clock bell rang,
the men began filing by the clock.

"What about the clock?"
I asked the man in charge.

"Didn't they give you a number?"
"No."

Then I told him my name, he gave
me a number and I punched out.

The boy was waiting for me
at the door.

"How'd you get the job?"
he asked curiously.

"Why, that was secured for me
before I showed up there,"
I answered.

"Who got it for you?" he asked.

"THAT SOMETHING,"
was my answer.

Something

is waiting for you.

"Aw," he answered, "quit your stringing me. How'd you get on. I seen a dozen men trying to get in on that work this morning, and they was all turned down."

"But," I explained with a smile, "they had never found 'THAT SOMETHING.'"

They ne
That Something

He again favored me
with the queer look.

"Say, where do you live?"
he asked finally.

"I am going to find a place now,"
I answered.

"Well, say" he cried,
"my maw keeps a boarding house,
and it's all right, too. Why don't
you come up to my place?"

There was but one other boarder.
He was a professor of a number
of "ology" branches at a nearby
denominational college.

He was a little man, with
unreasonable hair on his face,
and a very little on his head. He
wore thick glasses perched on a
beaked nose. His eyes were small
and black like shoe buttons.

He watched me covertly as I ate.

He's watching you...

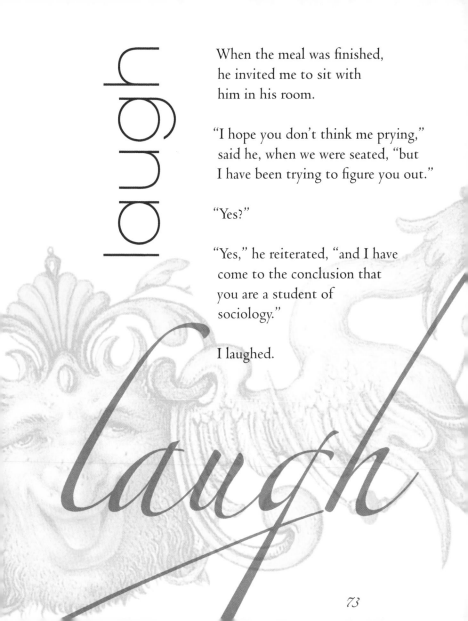

laugh

When the meal was finished, he invited me to sit with him in his room.

"I hope you don't think me prying," said he, when we were seated, "but I have been trying to figure you out."

"Yes?"

"Yes," he reiterated, "and I have come to the conclusion that you are a student of sociology."

I laughed.

what keeps the Underd down?

"Bobby tells us you are packing boxes at his store."

I nodded assent.

"Then," he said triumphantly, "of course, it is for the study for the conditions of the working masses that you are down there."

"Yes," I admitted, "I am very much interested in conditions of the masses right now."

"Then you can help me," he cried. "I am writing a series of papers on that very subject. Will you answer me this, please. What is it that keeps the underdog down? What is it that the upper ten possesses that the under ten thousand does not have?"

"Why, it's 'THAT SOMETHING,'" I answered.

mother

Love

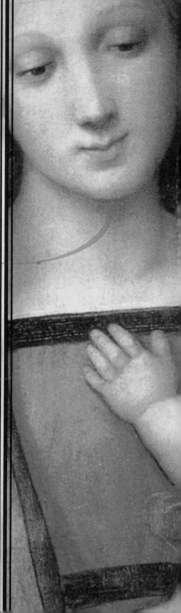

"What do you mean?
Education? Environment?"

Before my mind was flashed
the picture of my boyhood.

I saw my home,
I remembered the tender care
of my parents, the love of a mother,
the guiding hand of a father.

Guide

father

ויהי משה רועה ... בעשת רעושיש טער ורחלה הרק
... אמרו ... גם בן סוד מרש ועשה טיב כי מהחל
לעשיר החרש מנעגרין ... הונה ... הוה למחל
... במהם הגר גדל כמו שטול מוסר
... התירק רב בנעברין וכטישטור והרק
... ויחל להכיר הטוב והרע ... שיסנור
... ... הרשונים ... מעושבג ... הט

הָאִישׁ אֲשֶׁר וְלֹא הָלַךְ בַּעֲצַת
רְשָׁעִים וּבְדֶרֶךְ חַטָּאִים לֹא עָמָד
וּבְמוֹשַׁב לֵצִים לֹא יָשָׁב

78

אַשְׁרֵי ... אֶל לְשׁוֹן בִּלְשׁוֹן רַבִּים

I saw myself in college,
at the head of my class.

I remembered
that day when I was given
a sheet of parchment,
and was told that
I was a Master
of Arts.

שׁאַ אַ

Master

And then,
in the twinkling of an eye,
the scene changed,
and I saw that awful room,
with a hundred men lying
around me on the cold,
hard floor.

"No,"
I answered thoughtfully,
"it is neither of those things.

the scene

ange

'THAT SOMETHING'

is different entirely. I don't just know
what it is myself now, but I am going
to find it, pin it down and then
I will tell you more of it."

And as I looked into his face,
I noticed the same puzzled
expression as the boy
had worn.

And so, by mutual consent,
the subject was changed,
and we talked of trivial things.

And for a week or more
I packed boxes and drove nails.
I was a good packer.

I made **"THAT SOMETHING"**
work with me all the time.

82

f go
find it!

"Feel the real significance of what the great artists, the serious masters, tell us in their masterpieces, that leads to God; one man said it in a book; another in a picture."

Vincent Van Gogh

One day, I noticed the shipping clerk had ahead of him more than he could handle.

There were men in the department idle. They could do nothing until he checked up to them.

I laid down my hammer and walked over to where he stood.

"I am to help you this afternoon," I said simply. He looked up with a start. "Oh," he exclaimed. Then: "Well, that's good. I'm glad they have sense enough to give me somebody to help out at last."

olunteer

He handed me a bunch of papers, and made room for me at the desk.

The superintendent of the department was out of the room at the time. Presently he returned and glanced at me curiously.

"So they've got you helping out Dickey?" he asked.

I shrugged my shoulders without looking up, and continued figuring.

MAKE ROOM FOR OTHERS

When I left the room, that night,
the superintendent of the department
joined me.

"Say," he said, as we turned up the
street, "I never did just get on to how
you were put in there. What's the
idea? Working through to
learn the business?"

Help

without

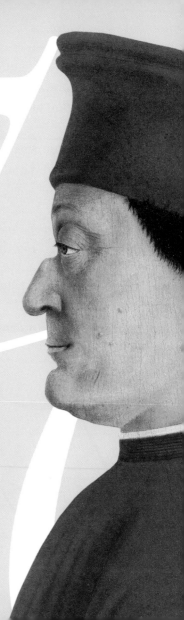

"Yes," I answered with confidence, "just that. I am to learn every detail of it."

"Well, I thought something of the kind. Which of 'em are you kin to?"

"I do not think it wise to discuss that at this time," was my answer.

"Oh sure," he hastened to say. "I don't mean to be inquisitive. Anything I can do to help you, let me know."

And then he left me.

hesitation

The shipping clerk
was a bright young fellow.

I liked him, and he liked me.

One day, shortly after I had received
my first raise in wages, he came
to me with a problem.

That night I stayed down with him
and we worked it out together.

We soon got in the habit of staying
down one night every week, and
working over his systems.

work it out
Together.

He lacked originality.
I helped him.

He had been doing things just like
the fellow before him had done them.

The business had been growing
rapidly—practically doubled.

We worked out an improved system.
We drew up forms. We planned
it out in every detail.

Be

Original

One day, he carried our plans to
the Man in Authority.

There came up a question that
the shipping clerk did not quite
understand. And so they
sent for me.

I was a well dressed man at this time.
Nothing flashy, nothing loud, but
well clothed. That had been my
first investment.

My approach was far different from
that of the sniveling beggar, who
had asked the man on the street
corner for food.

invest in

who are

The Man in Authority
looked at me in surprise.

"Who are you?"

I handed him my card.

These cards
were my second
investment.

He thumbed it
a moment in silence.

you are here
Temporarily

"You are packing boxes?"
he asked in surprise.

"I am in the packing room—
temporarily."

And then he went over the shipping
clerk's plans in detail.

"I think they're all right," said the
Man in Authority. "I'll have these
forms sent to the printer
in the morning."

As we turned to leave the office, he called me back. "How long have you been in the packing rooms?'

"Sixty-three days," I answered.

"You've been there long enough. There is nothing more for you to learn there, is there?"

"No."

FINIT PROLOGVS

THERE IS ALWAYS MORE TO LEARN.

captuf eft in peccatif
mbra tua . uiuem ingen
a edom qui ba SEN
te quoq; puenet calix
daberif . TAU
itaf tua filia syon · non
migrette · Visitauit ini
m · discoopuit peccata tua ·
ATIO IEREMIE P phe

TIO EIVSDEM :

ECORDARE
dne quid acciderit nob.
intuere & respice op
probrium nostrum ·
hereditas nra uersa
est ad alienos . domuf
nre ad extraneos ·
Pupilli facti sumuf
absq; patre · matref
nre quasi uidue ·
...uam bibimus & lig
...parauimus
...mur. lassif
...ef.
...anum & assyrii·
...ie·
...uerunt & non sunt·
...uum portauimus·
...t nri · & non sunt
...manu eorum·
...rebamuf panem
...deserto·
...anuf exusta est

linquef nof inlongitudinem dierum?
Conuerte nof dne adte conuertemur · in
noua dief nrof sicut aprincipio·
Sed piciens reppulisti nof · iratuf ef contra
nof uehementer FINIT ORATIO IEREMIE

INCIPIT PROLOGVS INLIBRV

BARVCH NOTARII IEREMIE Pphe

Liber iste qui baruch nomine pnotatur inhebreo
canone non habetur · sed tantum inuulgata editione. Si
militer & ecpta ieremie pphete · Propter notitiam autem
legentium hic scripta sunt · quia multa de xpo nouissimisq;
temporibus indicat·

FINIT PROLOGVS

De oratione & sacrificio prouita Nabuchodonosor·

INCP LIBB BARVCH FRR IEREMIE
PROPHE:
EL.
VERBA
LIBRI
QVE SCRIPSIT

baruch filiuf neeri · filii amasie · filii sedechie ·
filii sedei · filii helchie inbabylonia ~ inanno

discerning Eye

La folie surchauffée beugle dans la locomotive
La peste le choléra se lèvent comme des braises ardentes sur n
Nous disparaissons dans la guerre en plein dans un tunnel
La faim, la putain, se cramponne aux nuages en débandade
Et fiente des batailles en tas puants de morts
Fais comme elle, fais ton métier...

« Dis, Blaise, sommes-nous bien loin de M

Oui, nous le sommes, nous le sommes
Tous les boucs émissaires ont crevé dans ce désert

Entends les mauvaises cloches de ce troupeau galeux
Tomsk Tchéliabinsk Kainsk Obi Taïchet Verkne-Oudinsk Kourgane Samara F
La mort en Mandchourie
Est notre débarcadère est notre dernier repaire
Ce voyage est terrible
Hier matin
Ivan Oulitch avait les cheveux blancs
Et Kolia Nicolaï Ivanovitch se ronge les doigts depuis ... urs
Fais comme elles la Mort la Famine fais ton métier
Ça coûte cent sous, en transsibérien ça coûte cent f
Enfièvre les banquettes et rougeoie sous la table
Le diable est au piano
Ses doigts noueux excitent toutes les femmes
La Nature
Les Gonges
Fais ton métier
Jusqu'à Kharbine...

- Dis, Blaise, somme ... sin loin de Montmartre ?
- Non mais... fiche-moi la p
Ta as les hanches angulai
Ton ventre est aigre et tu as

C'est loin ce que Paris a e
C'est aussi un peu d'âme...

He studied me for a while in silence. "Funny neither of 'em has ever said anything about you to me," he said at length, speaking half to himself.

"I suppose the Old Man's idea was for you to work out your own salvation. Is that it?"

"In a way," I replied. "What any man accomplishes must eventually come from '**THAT SOMETHING**' within him."

...hments come from within.

He pondered this for a moment.
Then he scrawled a few words on
a piece of paper. "Hand that to
Perkins in the Auditing Department
tomorrow morning, and we'll see
how you show up there."

I thanked him,
and turned to leave the room.

"And say," calling me back the second
time, "Better forget about my having
said anything about your relations
with the Old Man. After all, you see,
it's none of my business."

"Certainly," I answered,
and left the room.

谢谢你

always say

Thank You

Dominica .i. quadrage
... inuocauit me ſime.
et ego exaudiam eū
...eripiam eum et glo

...nficabo eum longitud
dierū ...mplebo eū et
Qui hitat mad ps.
...utorio altiſſimu ī pro

Three months later,
I left Bob's mother's boarding house.

It hurt me to do this.
She had been almost a mother to me.

There was a home life about the place
that I had learned to love.

Even the little, hairy Ology Professor
and his fanciful theories
had become dear to me.

But **"THAT SOMETHING"**
demanded that I
move on.

Sometimes you
move on

And so I moved on up the hill.

I arranged for a small suite
of rooms at a quiet family hotel.

It was at the suggestion
of the Man in Authority
that I chose this hotel.

It was where he lived.

Choose

Suggestions

wisely.

Ab
au
us

Ab
au
ia

Pzoptnui
pamta

Pa
ui
us

Pa
ui
a

pauuel's
pmatren

bozum
filius
filia

Patruui
magñ aut
mag

Au
us

An
ia

Auuck's
magnus
o Attem
mag

bozum
filius fi
lia

ppiozr so
brui ppio
sobzina

Patruui
Amita

Pa
ter

Ma
ter

Auuck's
o Attem

ppioz so
brui ppio
sobzina

Soz
nepo
te

ff patuel
zamitunus

Frater

109

Sozor

Cosubrui

Nei

And so we became
at first acquaintances.

Then friends.

He urged that I join his club.
I made friends of the right sort there.

All of these things were investments.

And so the year rolled 'round.

become
friends

SPEAK

It was the time Perkins
took his vacation.

I was given the place
until he returned.

One day the Old Man came into
the office. He looked at me keenly.

Directly the Man in Authority
also came in. The Old Man called
him aside. I overheard a portion
of their conversation.

"Who's the man
at Perkins' desk?"
the Old Man asked.

The Man in Authority
mentioned my name.

"Funny I never heard of him before,"
said the Old Man.

The Man in Authority gasped.

AND THE REST
WAS SPOKEN

in guarded tones, and
I heard no word further.

IN GUARDED TONES

That night, the Man in Authority came into my sitting room.

"Say," he began, "you've certainly got me locoed or something. I thought you were a ward or a long lost cousin of the Old Man's. Now today he comes in and jumps on me about putting you in this place of responsibility without first knowing all about you. Of course, I know you're all right," he added kindly, "but by Jupiter, I'm placed in a deucedly unholy kind of a light anyway."

"What's all the trouble?" I asked. "My work going wrong?"

"I should say not," he exclaimed with enthusiasm, "but that's beside the point. What's got me going is *how the dickens you did it*. How you got to hold down the most responsible job on the works without anybody knowing just what you really are. Tell me about yourself, will you?"

did it!

"Well," I began in a sing-song voice, "I was born of poor but honest parents, in a quaint little hamlet of Virginia, where the rising sun—"

"Oh, drat the history and the rising sun. Tell me who you are kin to, or who is backing you up. It's the pull that counts, these days. Who gave you your start with the company?"

born where the Rising Sun

I never

Though

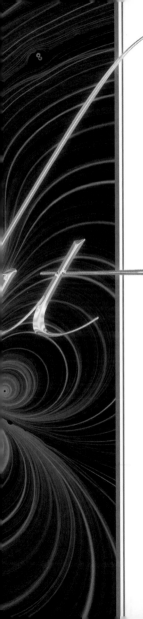

I leaned back
in my leather Morris chair.

Memory brought back the picture
of that drab day, of just a year before.

And that brought to my mind the
card that had been given to me.
I had not thought of it before
until that minute.

I arose, and went to the closet,
where hung the very suit I had worn
on that eventful day. I had kept it
as a souvenir of my awakening.

And, as I had hoped, the card
was in a pocket of the shabby vest.

For the first time, I read the name
engraved thereon.

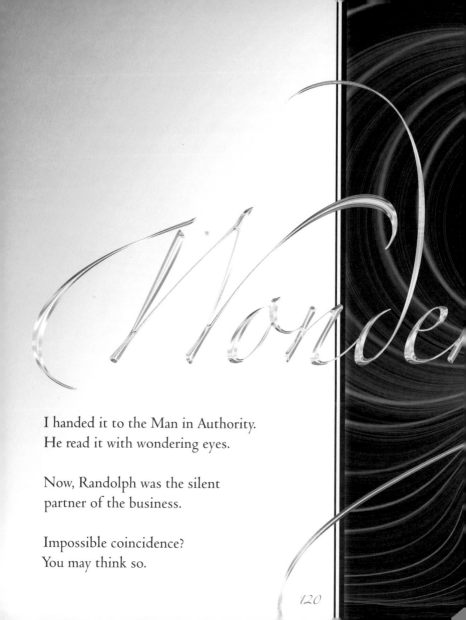

I handed it to the Man in Authority.
He read it with wondering eyes.

Now, Randolph was the silent
partner of the business.

Impossible coincidence?
You may think so.

ing eyes

read with

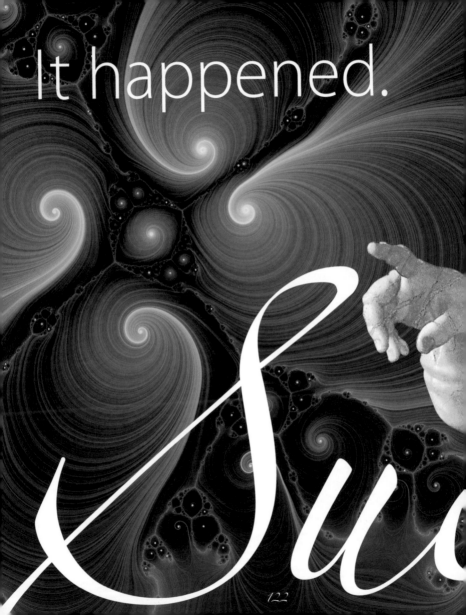

It happened.

Su

I know men who believe
success is impossible.

And to them success 'IS' impossible.

And so, perhaps,
you believe this impossible.

But I tell you it happened.

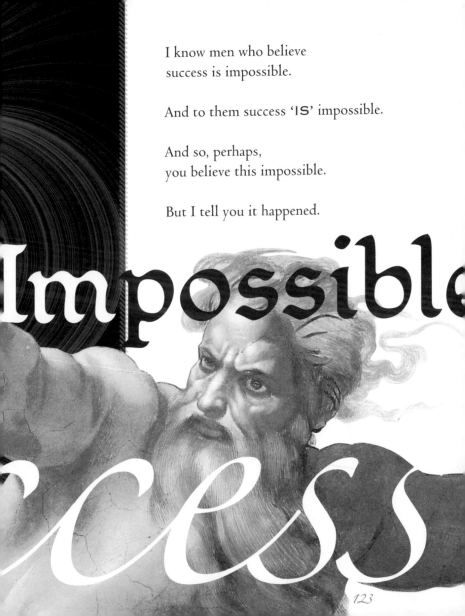

Impossible

ccess

la Musique du Silence

we don't always know

Why

"Funny Randolph never mentioned
 your name to the Old Man,"
 the Man in Authority was saying.
"Anyway, I wish I'd known this when
 he was talking about you today."

"I'm glad you didn't," I answered
 with a short laugh.

"Why?" he asked puzzled.

"Go there to the phone and call
 up Randolph. I think he'll
 tell you why."

"But——," he began.

"Go on and call him up.
 I want you to," I insisted.

Le Livre

instrument spirituel.

watch them change.

In a moment,
Randolph was on the line.

"Ask him," I insisted.
The Man in Authority did so.

I watched
the changing expressions
on his face.

"You - say - you - never - heard -
of - the man!" gasped the Man in
Authority. "Why, he's holding down
the most responsible job in the place."

"Better let me talk to Mr. Randolph,"
I interrupted.

His hand was trembling
as he surrendered the phone.

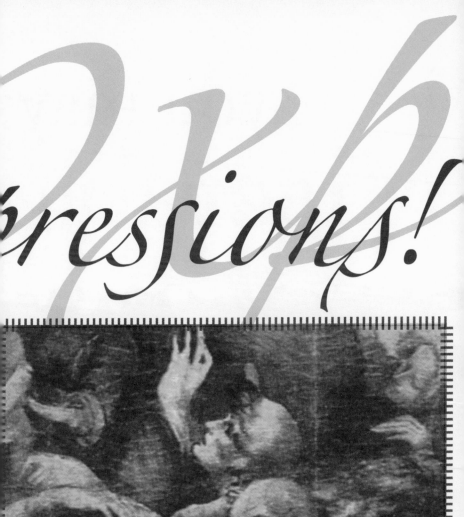

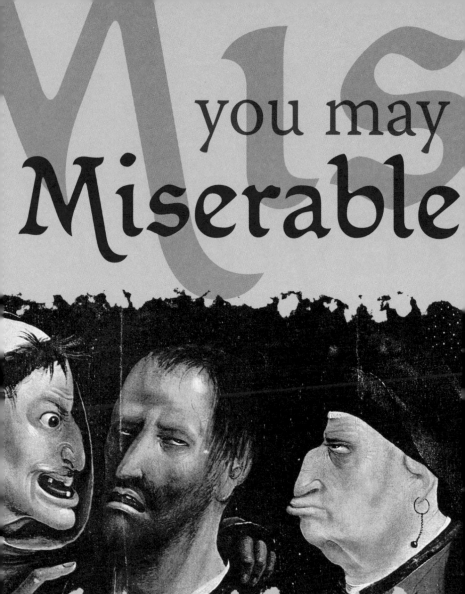

you may

Miserable

remember that *era* Day

"Mr. Randolph," I said, "I know you do not remember my name, for I am quite sure you have never heard it.

You may, however, remember one miserable day, a year ago, when a beggar asked you for food."

"Well, go on,"
came a crisp voice over the phone.

"You may also remember telling
that beggar that it was not food he
needed. You told him that it was
'THAT SOMETHING.'

I have learned to use it, and I want
to thank you for having shown
me the way. When may I have
the opportunity of telling
you about it?"

I want to

thank You

Just what is that ething?

An hour later, the story you have just
heard was told to a strange trio:
the Man in Authority,
the Professor of Ologies
and Matthew Morrison Randolph

From time to time, as I told the
tale, Randolph nodded his head in
approval, and I noticed a strange light
begin to glow in the little professor's
eyes. When I had finished, we sat for
a long time in silence, broken at last
by Randolph, who said:

"And now tell me just what you think
'THAT SOMETHING' really is?"

SCS JOHS

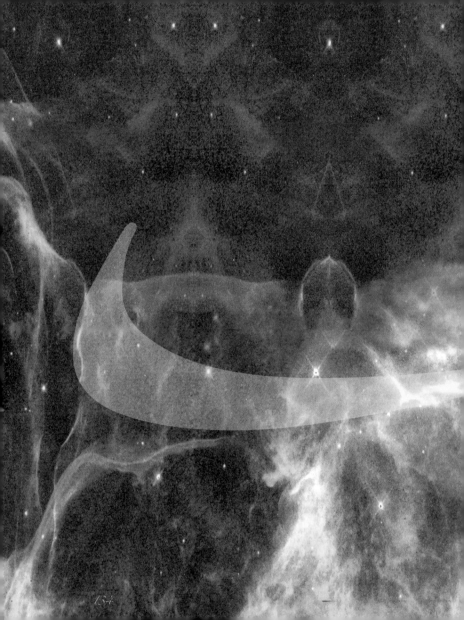

It is Power

I shook my head in dismay. "You folks know as much as I do about it," I answered. "But of this one thing I am convinced, through and through. It is real **POWER**, as truly real as the electric current.

It is the power of the inner man, the fuel of the soul machine.

It is the one thing necessary.

We are all of us born much alike.
We come into the world, all animals
of a type. All of us have the senses,
equally developed. And then we
begin to live, animals all.

Until we wake
'**THAT SOMETHING**' of the soul,
we live as a horse lives. We bear on
our muscle those that have found
'**THAT SOMETHING**.'

And we bear on them on up the
mountain, to take their places
among the masters.

Re

4

when you

awaken

aissance

'THAT SOMETHING'

lies dormant in every soul until
aroused. With many, it sleeps until
the last great sleep.

Sometimes it does not wake
until man stands tottering on
the border of the grave.

Sometimes it is found by the child,
playing by its mother's knee.

Some men have sneered,
and called it Luck.

Luck is but the fleeting smile
of Fortune.

within you

is a

Fortune

'THAT SOMETHING'
is the highway to her home.

A man's success depends alone on
'THAT SOMETHING'
of his SOUL.

Abraham Lincoln found it when a lad.
It added light to the flickering glow
of the wood fire, that he might
see to read. It spurred him on,
and on, and on.

your success
depends on that

ething

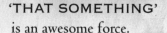

'THAT SOMETHING'
is an awesome force.

It made of a puny Corsican
the Ruler of the World!

It made of a thin-chested
bookkeeper the money king
of a great country!

It made Edison
the great man of his age!

That Something

within you is

wesome!

It made Carnegie!
It made Woodrow Wilson!
It made Roosevelt!

It can make YOU!

And it is NOW in YOUR Soul!

Awake it—now!
'THAT SOMETHING.'"

Wake it

Vow!

Foo
ske

Again the silence followed.

I watched the Professor of Many Ologies. I saw the kindled fires in his eyes gradually die out. He shook his head wearily.

"No, it can't be done; it can't be done," he murmured. "I have drunk deeply of the cup of life, and I am now drinking of the dregs. The cup is filled but once, and when it's gone, there's nothing left but the dregs of old age and poverty."

"You fool!" cried Randolph, leaning forward and shaking the little man roughly.

"You almost had
'THAT SOMETHING'
in your power, and now you sing
it back to sleep with your silly
song of pessimism.

It's the false philosophy, that such
as you sing, which has kept men
in the ruts of their own digging
for centuries past.

Wake, man, wake!

Wake
'THAT SOMETHING'
within your soul!"

The two men sat looking deeply into each other's eyes. It was the little man who broke the silence.

"Thank you, Randolph," he said quietly. "You are right. I will!"

Then Randolph turned to me. "Man, write that story you've told us. Write it so that everyone may read. Send that message out into the world. If people will read that story, read and reread, until it is written on their memories, if they will believe the message you bring, and then if they will but *awake that something within their souls that now lies asleep* — I say if you can help people do this, you will have done more for mankind than anyone or any thousand men have done in many, many years.

"Write it, man, write it word for word as you have told it here, so that everyone may read. Write it, man, write it!"

And so it has been written.

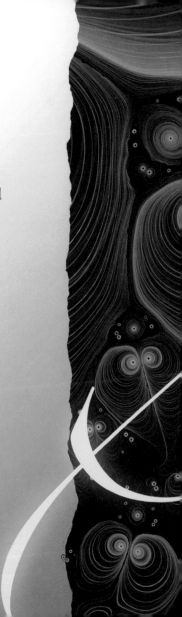

Share

your awakening!

And you
who have read it through,
I pray that you may read every
word again and again, until

"THAT SOMETHING"

of your soul has been aroused,
and you have taken your places
among the Rulers of the World.

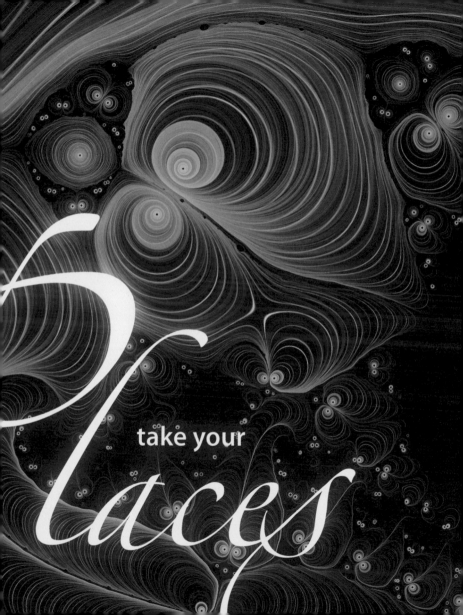

take your

The End

which is the

eginning

Our Awakening
will come when we let go
of our egos and open our hearts
to a higher level of Awareness.

One of the first signs
of our Awakening will be
a Renaissance of iconic books.

An iconic book is a gift from God
and a gateway to our Awakening.

This book was designed by
Martin Alberti.

About William Woodbridge

William Witherspoon Woodbridge, the author of *That Something*, was the gifted writer of a series of short novels that revolutionized the lives of countless individuals in the early 1900s. Woodbridge is also the author of *Something More, Scooting Skyward*, and *Bradford, You're Fired!* These stories gained widespread recognition from many of the prominent leaders and dignitaries of the time. Thomas Edison remarked, "I have read *That Something*. It tells the *whole* story."

That Something was a key influence on Napoleon Hill, whose *Think and Grow Rich* became one of the best selling books of all time. Paul J. Meyer, the author and pioneer of the self-improvement industry whose programs have sold more than two billion dollars worldwide, attributes much of his success to his ability to harness William Woodbridge's *That Something* and make it work for him.